THE **POWER** OF
HEALTHY ESTEEM

The Power of Healthy Esteem

THE POWER OF HEALTHY ESTEEM

Renee Fowler Hornbuckle

Unless otherwise indicated, all Scriptures quotations are taken from the King James Version or the New International Version of the Bible

The Power of Healthy Esteem
Copyright © 2001
Revised Version & Reprinted in 2012
Renee Fowler Hornbuckle
www.reneehornbuckle.org

Library of Congress Catalog – in Publication Data

ISBN 978-1481206907

Printed in the United States of America

Published by Jabez Books
(A Division of Clark's Consultant Group)
www.clarksconsultantgroup.com

All rights reserved. No part of this book may be reproduced, stored in a retrieval system, or transmitted in any form or by any means, electronic, mechanical photocopying, recording, or otherwise, without written consent of the publisher except in the case of brief quotations in critical articles or reviews.

Success--Religious aspects—Self-Esteem –Christianity

Thank You!
You are all loved and appreciated!

My Family for their unwavering support.

My true friends who stood beside me and
encouraged me every step of the way.

My Congregation and Community who by standing with me
forced me to not give up and stand up for what was right.

The host of
Ministers, Counselors and Life Coaches who helped me heal,
advised me and gave insight to this project.

And to the Women and Men who have allowed me to minister
to them and who shared their stories. This is what truly gave me
the courage to step up and share mine!

Love you all more!

Table of Contents

Introduction   11

Chapter 1: What is This Power Thing?   13

Chapter 2: What is Self-Image?   23

Chapter 3: What is Esteem?   27

Chapter 4: What is Self-Esteem?   33

Chapter 5: What is Healthy Esteem?   39

Chapter 6: Do I Have Negative Esteem Or Healthy Esteem?   43

Chapter 7: How Do I Develop Healthy Esteem?   57

Chapter 8: The Power of Healthy Esteem?   65

Introduction

While we are here on earth, it is important for us to understand our purpose. Our purpose can be multifaceted. However, our main purpose is to love God, to make Him known to others, and to glorify Him in all that we do. God saw fit to ordain our lives from the very beginning. At this beginning, we were empowered with unique abilities and giftings (that only we have been given) to demonstrate God's love and expression to the world. When the right time came, God allowed those unique abilities and giftings to be released into the earth realm (when you were born), so that His kingdom would be established here on earth. In other words, God placed greatness inside of you before you were even born, and it is His intent that you utilize the greatness (power) that He gave you!

If we are to utilize this greatness (power) in all that we do, then we must have the confidence and assurance of knowing who we are. Often this can appear to be a very difficult task because in our day-to-day lives it may seem that much of what we are experiencing is not something that seems so great. But in essence it really is great, and as we focus on our God-given purpose, regardless of our circumstances in life, we should see the wonderful future awaiting us. God is simply preparing us to be the vessels that He so predestined us to be. We must acknowledge the fact that we have come into the kingdom for such a time as this to fulfill our responsibility to what it is that God desires for our lives. God desires us to be healthy and whole! He desires for us to understand that we are fearfully and wonderfully made! He desires for us to have healthy esteem! He also desires for us to fulfill great purpose and to make a difference in the world in which we live!

After reading this book you will be challenged to take on the healthy esteem that God desires for you to have so that you can be all that God has called you to be. Just know that as you start this journey, it is my intent to share with you God's perfect plan for YOU to operate with POWER in your life so that you can accomplish great things and have success!

Chapter One

What is This Power Thing?

As we go through life, we often hear words like "power," "self-esteem," and "empowerment." These are inspirational and motivational words, but do we really understand what these words mean? When I was a young girl, I equated words such as "power" to super heroes. And I defined words like self-esteem, with my parents' guidance, as being self-assured of who I was as a person. As I matured, especially during the onset of the feminist movement, I understood the word "power" to be utilized as another term for rights. Now that I am wiser, and I have an understanding of what true power is, I know that "power" is not another term for "super heroes" or to define "rights," but it is so much more.

So what is POWER? The definition of power according to the dictionary is *the ability or capacity to perform or act effectively; it is the energy or motive force by which a thing is operated; having influence over.*

You might be saying to yourself, "what does this have to do with my life?" It has a lot to do with your life and how you live. You must begin to understand that God has empowered you with His Spirit, thereby enabling you to have the ability or capacity to be productive and effective in life. What each of us is empowered with is the same power Jesus used when he walked the earth, and it is the same power He wants you to operate in each day. The same spiritual energy and motive force that He displayed when He lived on earth ought to be displayed through you as you walk in the earth realm each day. God has left a mighty counselor (the power of the Holy Spirit) to dwell within you so that you can be empowered to be His representative. I think it's comforting to have a power other than ourselves to rely on to see us through this life.

Understanding Empowerment

So, how does this empowerment work in our lives? The Holy Spirit lives inside the Christian and guides the actions of those who desire His presence. The Holy Spirit empowers the Christian to step outside his comfort zone to do extraordinary acts of faith for God. Being filled with the Spirit involves transforming our minds to the mind of Christ as we engage in spiritual activities. Walking in the Spirit leads to a sense of peace and joy, as we partner with God in His glorious plans.

Billy Graham, one of the greatest evangelists who ever lived, explained in his book, one of the best and most comprehensive explanations I believe of the Holy Spirits power. **Excerpt from "Does the Holy Spirit Shine Through You?"** by Billy Graham

> *It is impossible to understand the Bible, Christian living, the structure of the church, or our own relationship with God without understanding the Person and work of the Holy Spirit. The Holy Spirit is not an "it." The Holy Spirit is a person. The Bible says that He is not something. He is Someone. He is God.*
>
> *There are three persons in the Trinity— God the Father, God the Son, God the*

Holy Spirit. The Bible teaches that the Holy Spirit is all-powerful. We read in Micah 3:8, "I am full of power by the Spirit of the Lord" (NKJV). The Bible says that God is present everywhere. No matter where we go, He is there. "Where can I go from Your Spirit? Or where can I flee from Your presence?" (Psalm 139:7, NKJV). The Holy Spirit can be in your heart and my heart, and we may live a thousand miles apart.

The Holy Spirit has all knowledge. The Bible says, "The Spirit searches all things, even the deep things of God" (1 Corinthians 2:10). It is the Holy Spirit who teaches us and takes us deeper into God's truth as we go along in our Christian life. We are to grow in the grace and knowledge of Christ, but we can grow only by the help of the Holy Spirit.

The moment that we receive Christ as Savior, the Holy Spirit comes to live in our heart. Our Body becomes the temple of the Holy Spirit, and the Holy Spirit helps us live the Christian life.

There is not a person anywhere who can be a Christian without the Holy

Spirit. There is not a person who can follow Christ without the help of the Holy Spirit. The Holy Spirit sees everything that goes on. He knows what goes on in our hearts. He knows what goes on in our minds. Nothing is hidden from Him.

And the Bible says that the Holy Spirit is eternal. In Hebrews 9:14, we read "the eternal Spirit."

The Holy Spirit is called holy. The Bible says, "Be holy, because I am holy" (1 Peter 1:16). One of the Holy Spirit ministries is to help make us holy. We ought to be more holy today than we were yesterday. We should always be conforming more to the image of Jesus Christ, and it is the Holy Spirit who helps us in this growing process.

So in order to be empowered, we must cooperate with the Holy Spirit and allow the Holy Spirit to be a part of our Christian life. Our growth and development can use the help and guidance of the Holy Spirit in order for us to reach our full potential. "The Spirit helps us in our weakness" (Romans 8:26).

I love studying words. In some words, prefixes are placed at the beginning of a word to modify or change its meaning. The prefix *em* means – to put into; within; to cover or provide with; to cause to be; thoroughly; often used as an intensive.

Anytime this prefix (em) is added to a word, it is used to intensify. So, it is safe to say that the word *empowered* simply means intense power. So in being empowered as a person, you need to understand the magnitude of what this word (empowered) represents.

Empowered - to invest especially with legal power; to grant authority or power to.

So if God left you the power of the Holy Spirit. You are an authorized ambassador charged with the responsibility of representing Him here on earth. You have the power to decree laws, fulfill commands, and arrest injustices. God knows it and Satan knows it. The question is: Do you know that "you have got the power?" You will not be able to perform at your highest potential nor will you be effective until this truth is resonant in your heart.

Stability vs. Ability

God is trying to get you to walk in the divine full authority that He intended for your life. He has provided everything that is necessary for you to excel. Over many years of counseling, I have found the greatest tragedy in the lives of people is the lack of mental stability. The individuals I counsel are bright, young, vivacious, and intelligent. Their achievements are many and their education par excellence, yet they sit in my office and cry because they do not feel empowered. Though they may have natural power on their jobs, that nagging voice of unworthiness argues with them when they are alone. These individuals have the mental ability to achieve greatness, yet they settle for mediocrity. I have come to the conclusion that in order to fill the void, you can get this true power only through studying the Word of God, by identifying who God says you are, and learning that HE has empowered you to walk in dominion and authority.

Are you acting effectively in all that you do? Effectiveness is a result of stable thinking based on godly principles and not on mental ascension or humanistic education. In your thinking, you must have a stable mind. If you are going to be effective in your mind, ask God to come in and empower you in your mind so that you will have the power to be stable and not tossed to and fro. If you are unstable in your mind, it is inevitable that you will be unstable in everything that you do.

James 1:8, "A double minded man is unstable in all his ways."

Look at Me – Do I like What I See?

John 1:22 Amplified Bible (AMP), *"Then they said to him, Who are you? Tell us, so that we may give an answer to those who sent us. What do you say about yourself?*

Nicole came into my office one day just to "talk." Absolutely beautiful! Cheerleader, varsity team member, honor student – everything seemed like a "perfect" person would be. Today, she was holding back a secret, one that she would be too ashamed to tell. If she told, her enemies would gloat and her peers would scoff. Finally, she revealed that she was pregnant, and the father had skipped town. Furthermore, she had met him in a most remote place – a place that good girls like her avoided. Her world was falling apart. It was at this point that the Lord and I stepped in. In her frenzy, I dared to ask her, "What do you think of yourself?" She struggled with answers, and the ones she muttered all had to do with what others thought of her. She had built a life of accepting what others thoughts of her to the point of wanting to abort the baby so her image in their eyes would not be tainted.

In dealing with the power of healthy esteem, you must come face to face with your perception of yourself; rather than with the perceived perceptions that others have of you. In the Bible passage above, take note that they did not ask Jesus what others thought about Him, although it was mentioned. They questioned His take on Himself. Anytime we pause to take a look at ourselves, it reflects a true picture of who it is that we really are. This is typically not something that we really enjoy doing in the busyness of our day-to-day functions.

We do not want to pause and to stop, because quite often what happens is that we realize our inadequacies and our weaknesses. That is when certain negative things can come in and overtake us. Because of this, we tend to busy ourselves, not with the affairs of the Lord, but with stuff. Do you purposely fill your day with stuff because if you pause or slow down you are afraid that you will catch up with the real you?

For years I was fearful of slowing down because I knew I would have to face the real me. When I began to look at the real me I found I had some character flaws that needed work. I looked at myself and began to make the changes necessary so I could become healthy and whole.

You must learn to look yourself square in the mirror and deal with what is in you. Many of us may find that we do not like who we really are. However, that is when we need to be ready to work so that we are conformed to the image of Christ. We must begin to understand that God desires to empower, strengthen, and equip us with the power of the Holy Spirit. It is necessary for us as Christians to acknowledge the fact that we must be empowered in order to walk in the fullness of what God has for us.

Chapter Two

What is Self-Image?

Self-Image – an individual's conception of oneself in their own identity, abilities, and worth.

Self image is what we think and how we feel about ourselves. What is your view of yourself? How do you conceptualize your abilities? How do you conceptualize your values? How is it that you paint a picture of yourself?

Martha in the Bible is an example of a poor self-image. In Luke 10:38-41, we see how Martha got caught up in what she did.

Luke 10:38-41 Amplified Bible (AMP)

38 Now while they were on their way, it occurred that Jesus entered a certain village, and a woman named Martha received and welcomed Him into her house.

39 And she had a sister named Mary, who seated herself at the Lord's feet and was listening to His teaching.

40 But Martha [overly occupied and too busy] was distracted with much serving; and she came up to Him and said, Lord, is it nothing to You that my sister has left me to serve alone? Tell her then to help me [to lend a hand and do her part along with me]!

41 But the Lord replied to her by saying, Martha, Martha, you are anxious and troubled about many things.

Guess what? You are not what you do! Many times we get so busy working that when the Lord speaks to us, we do not hear Him. Martha wanted Jesus to pity her. Her poor image caused her to be upset with her sister. She put her worth in her work instead of the Word. Do you find yourself criticizing others often? Are you always looking for someone to feel sorry for you? Is there a tendency to get jealous of other people? Do you feel inadequate if you do not have the right job title or position? If the answer is yes to any of these questions, then you might have a poor self-image.

What is it that you allow others to speak into your life that affects your ability to really see yourself the way that God intends for you to be? Ruth and Orpah were examples of women who allowed one woman to speak into their lives, and it changed their history. Orpah allowed Naomi to convince her that there was no future if she stayed with her. Naomi gave a compelling argument, but I believe Naomi was in a state of mourning when she gave this talk. Instead of comforting her, Orpah left. Ruth took a different approach; she knew her destiny was with Naomi. She recognized that she must cling to Naomi regardless of what Naomi said or what her sister did.

When you have low esteem, people can talk you out of your destiny. When you have healthy esteem, you are confident in your decisions. You know what you must do, and no one can cause you to change your mind.

At another point, Ruth had an opportunity to allow Naomi to speak into her life positively. She listened, because she knew it was God speaking through her. She had a powerful destiny and because her confident image allowed her to discern when God was talking. Sometimes our self-image is so bad we take any advice from anyone. You must know the direction God has for you and be confident! (Ruth)

Chapter Three

What is Esteem?

Esteem is a very interesting word.

Esteem – to regard highly or favorably; regard with respect or admiration; to consider as of a certain value or a certain type.

I find it quite interesting that a lot of times when we are searching to uncover our identity, we go on a mad journey to understand how we can go through a process of developing better esteem. If you look at the definition of the word, it already has to do with respect and admiration. We have to stop running to every meeting, prophet, and magazine trying to uncover what it is that our esteem should be. I know many of us get the fashion and glamour magazines and go through the "esteem test" to see if we have positive or negative esteem. However, what we must understand is that those things are based on the world's perspective of what esteem should be. We now live in an age where everyone is trying to get in touch with their spirituality. We see it on all the daytime television shows and reality shows because people are recognizing that there is something lacking, but you will not find it in a magazine, on a television program, or in the opinions of others. The only place that you are going to find your esteem is in the Word of God.

Low esteem is something that is present with most people during this era in the wake of unemployment and difficult times. I can recall years ago when we as women and members of various ethnic groups were fighting for certain issues and equality. We felt that if we were considered equal on certain levels, in our careers and other things, we would have more esteem and more value. But I really think that is something the enemy uses to come back and haunt us. Now that we are actually able to make higher incomes, have the power positions, and do and be whoever and whatever we want to, many of us are out of balance. Because we are out of balance, we have lost touch with who we really are.

Your conception (the way that you value yourself, your view of your work) is directly correlated to your value or your esteem. In the book of I Samuel, chapter 25 there is a story about a woman named Abigail who was married to an evil man. And no doubt he was probably constantly spewing out negative verbiage in their home. However, Abigail did not allow this to affect her self-esteem. She was able to portray a positive self-value, which enabled her to save her whole household.

Many people in relationships, although very beautiful or handsome, often end up with the wrong partner. They start to listen to what people say about them instead of knowing what God has to say, and because of this many people end up with low esteem. Not Abigail, she recognized God's anointing and used her wisdom to change her situation. God got rid of the fool in her life and gave her a king (I Samuel 25)!

I mentioned earlier that who you are is not what you do. Could it be that what we actually thought was so good has backfired? Has it now caused us to take on so much that we are out of touch with who we really are and who God created us to be?

This is not to say that I do not believe there are certain things that we should have fought for because God is not a respecter of persons. I just know that the balance in society had to come. God created us both (men and women) a little bit lower than the angels so there was immediate value and worth placed upon our lives. Could it be that we have lost sight of our value and esteem in our fight and our search?

If you look at some of the greatest women in the Bible as an example, they did not need to fight men for their esteem. On the contrary, they depended on their God-given abilities to create a life of success, prosperity, and holiness. Lydia was known as a God-fearing woman. She was very prominent in the business community. She influenced Paul to stay at her house, and following her lead, her whole household was saved. Instead of working against Paul, her esteem allowed her to work with him for the kingdom (Acts 16).

All Christians, especially women, need to put into perspective what is occurring now that we have taken on added responsibilities. Most of us have accepted defining ourselves by what we do and not by who we are. You should not be defined by what you do, but by who you are. Unfortunately, this is where the struggle begins.

Ask God to unveil your esteem level to you. As He reveals your current level of esteem, whether it is high esteem or low esteem, my prayer is that you personally take ownership and go to work on what it is that the Lord is speaking to you. God desires each of us to have healthy esteem.

What did God reveal to you about your esteem?

Chapter Four

What is Self-Esteem?

Self-esteem – self-respect; either positive or negative; the opinion that we hold of ourselves. Notice the word self-esteem. It is your view of yourself, your opinion of who you are. Remember, esteem means to regard highly or favorably, to regard with respect or admiration. If you add the word self, then self-esteem becomes the esteem that should reflect favorably upon your life when you look at who you are. Our self-esteem is constantly being affected by our own thinking, which can alter our reflection of ourselves.

The Bible tells a story of two prostitutes, Rahab and Gomer. They both started off with low self-esteem, but their lives turned out very differently. In the Book of Hosea, the Lord used Gomer as an example of Israel's unfaithfulness. Although Hosea (a prophet of God) married her, she continued her adulterous lifestyle. She ended up being a slave who was redeemed for half the value of a woman. She no doubt returned to her former way of life because she did not believe that she deserved better. Her actions were an obvious reflection of herself.

We find Rahab in the Book of Joshua. She lived in a city of people who did not know God. Recognizing that God was with the Israelites, Rahab made a decision that changed her destiny. Even though other people in Jericho considered her worthless, she had enough esteem one night to believe God. When Joshua and God's people pointed to her value and worth, Rahab changed the reflection that she saw of herself. As a result, she was honored and empowered by being in the genealogy of Jesus Christ.

Our belief system or self-esteem is formed by the opinions of others. If you take an evaluation of your own life and really look at the words that were spoken over you in your upbringing, you will begin to immediately identify your esteem level. You will see how people responded to you and how what they spoke over you is tied to your view or your opinion of yourself today. When other people transfer their beliefs to you, whether positive or negative, then that helps to form your opinion of yourself. It is up to you to decide whom you will and will not listen to.

Another danger that affects our self-esteem is when we compare ourselves to others. Typically, if we have low esteem, we start comparing ourselves to other people, which can eventually result in our having spirits of anger, envy, and jealousy. Others of us are so insecure with who we are that we become busybodies, and as the Bible would call it, "silly women (or men too for purposes of illustration)," who are weak and not strong enough to reject lies.

The enemy knows that he can capitalize on the minds of people, especially when they dwell on their inadequacies, sins, and carry guilt. If this state of mind continues, the enemy knows that he can enter the households of our minds, captivate us with untruths, and launch us to attack others.
2 Timothy 3:6, "For among them are those who enter into households and captivate weak women

weighed down with sins, led on by various impulses" (NAS).

---

1 Timothy 5:13 Contemporary English Version (CEV), "Besides, they will become lazy and get into the habit of going from house to house. Next, they will start gossiping and become busybodies, talking about things that are none of their business."

Our goal as brothers and sisters in Christ should be to love God, love ourselves, and then love one another. I should not compare myself to you. I can learn from you, I can sit at your feet and be taught, but I should not compare myself to you to the point that it makes me envious and jealous of what it is that God is doing in your life. A lot of times we feel we cannot receive wisdom, instruction and knowledge from certain people, and we blame our lack of receptivity on the person. But our receiving really does not have anything to do with that person; it has to do with how we feel internally, so we have to take responsibility for our own self-esteem.

You must recognize that your self-image sets the stage for your entire life. It is God's desire that you have a good image. He created you in His image, so He wants you to have a good image of yourself. Instead, all of these other factors and negative things that have affected us have set the course and the direction of our lives. That is why you must purpose in your heart that if you do not like where you are you must be willing to do the things that are necessary to change to be on God's plan. Otherwise, you will continue to stay in the image of your life that was presented to you, and all of us have room for improvement.

It should become a daily journey, a daily goal for you to want to improve your esteem and your life situations. Get away from people who think they are perfect and think that they do not need to change anything. It is your responsibility to make sure that you set yourself on the path to becoming the person you desire to be. You must learn to set the power that is within yourself free by believing in yourself.

In conclusion, let us briefly examine the lives of two queens: Esther "star" and Jezebel "Baal exalts." Both of these women were stars in their own right. They both were prominent political figures, wealthy, intelligent, and highly esteemed. They also knew how to command respect from their audiences and they knew how to gain what they desired. The only difference was in their self-esteem. Jezebel's lack of a healthy esteem caused her to do a variety of foolish things. She always had to command respect with a threat – a major sign of insecurity. She manipulated, while Esther entreated. Esther knew she could not be denied, while Jezebel feared she would be denied. Jezebel was very selfish and self-centered. She took away a man's land and his heritage in order to seek approval from her husband. She was in the emasculating business, emasculating males or females. Jezebel was the master of humiliation and degradation (I Kings 16). In contrast, Esther understood perfectly who she was and fervently built up the esteem of others, unselfishly sacrificing for the benefit of her nation. Here were two monarchs, two women, both of whose actions were a direct result of who they understood themselves to be. Which are you? Are you so insecure that you have to take from others, or are you confident enough to give of yourself?

Chapter Five

What is Healthy Esteem?

Through obtaining healthy esteem, things will become balanced in your life. Healthy self-esteem is how a person evaluates his or her own worth. It usually covers beliefs, emotions and the capacity to develop strong and powerful respect and confidence.

---

3 John 1:2, "Dear Friends, I pray for good fortune in everything you do, and for your good health—that your everyday affairs prosper, as well as your soul!"

The word health means to be sound in body. It also means to be sound in mind and spirit. Your good health should bring good words. It should bring doctrine and soundness in the faith. In the Greek, the word 'prosper' means to succeed in reaching.

So it is in line with God's Word that you will have prosperity in all of your actions. In other words, there is a progressive state of success and well-being that you should achieve in your lifetime. Spiritually, physically, emotionally, and materially, God desires for you to prosper. That is why you cannot compare yourself to anybody else. You have to know that what God has for you is just for you! Your part in this is to love others as you love God, as well as loving yourself, and to be obedient and committed to the Word of God. Honestly speaking, a lot of people often do not love themselves, because they do not pursue a love relationship with God. They pant after His provision as a drug addict would cocaine. Let's set the record straight starting now. You are commanded to love God because He first loved you.

Because God knows the plans He has for you, it is important to seek Him daily. Once you do this, you will find that it is just fine for you to succeed in everything that you put your hand to as long as it lines up with the Word of God. You will reach every level that God desires for you if you continually study His Word to show yourself approved.

The noble character of the Proverbial 31:10, woman is an example of what God has available for us. She feared God, which was the first step on her journey of success. She was a powerful woman with a thriving business. She was a profitable investor and an excellent home manager. She received the respect of her husband and family. Through her blessings, she was able to help others. She was healthy! So whether you are male or female, when you are healthy in your self-esteem you will prosper in all aspects of your life.

It takes extremely healthy esteem to lead a nation. In a time when it was rare to see women in leadership positions, Deborah led Israel. She did not let being female stop her from reaching the destiny and purpose God had for her, but she had to be convinced that God's confidence in her and her value to Him were enough to launch her into her purpose (Judges, chapters 4 & 5).

Therefore, to achieve healthy esteem, you must decide for yourself that you are willing and ready to progress to a state of well being. The "power" is activated in your life when you desire and are willing to move forward in God's plan for your life. God desires us to be successful! God desires that our well being be stable! God wants us healthy!

Healthy esteem is found in individuals who have accepted themselves as God's unique masterpiece. They are confident and willing to let others shine, because they know in God's eyes they are irreplaceable and unforgettable. They have the power over their mind, their past, and their beliefs. They choose to dare to believe God and think good! I know that if you have reached this far in the book, you too are on your way to being a godly person of power with healthy esteem!

Chapter Six

Do I have Negative Esteem or Healthy Esteem?

People with negative esteem typically:

- ❖ **Suffer from identity crises.** They are constantly in a state or period of psychological distress. They are confused as to their goals and priorities. When you suffer from an identity crisis, you always seek a clearer sense of self, and tend to accept the negative role that people speak upon you in society because you are constantly searching. For example, Barak did not feel he could win the battle without Deborah, a confident person, going with him (Judges, chapter 5). He saw Deborah as more anointed with a better connection to God. As a result, he never got the complete glory God desired to give him. Instead he shared his glory with Deborah.

- **Begin to blame others for their failures.** You do not have time to blame others for your failure. You must take responsibility and ownership for what His Word says for your life. A person with low self-esteem does not feel worthy. People who boast in the name of the Lord and are confident in who He has called them to be, but take this confidence to the next level of arrogance, do not have positive esteem. Positive esteem is when you can confidently know who your Father is, know who He created you to be, and know and understand His plan for your life. Adam is a prime example. He blamed Eve, who blamed the serpent (Genesis 3). Living an unholy life is a breeding ground for poor self-esteem. Notice that when you live righteously before God, a confidence is present in everything you do because you are secure.

- ❖ **Have an unrealistic sense of their strengths and weaknesses.** Typically, if people have low self-esteem, they will only focus on things that they are comfortable doing. They have a false sense of their strengths and weaknesses, and they will never be able to speak to the good that God placed within them. God empowers you. God placed His image within you. If you are ever going to break the pattern, then you have to acknowledge that if you never have anything good to say about anything, you have to change. The list could go on. Look at Moses, "I cannot speak" (Exodus 4). He did not look at his courage, his training, his heritage, or even God's goodness in sparing him. He looked at one human impediment rather than all of the other things God saw. Jeremiah said, "I am but a child," Gideon asked, "Who am I?" and the list goes on. Our human tendency is to look at what is not there rather than what is there. We must learn to look at what is there.

- ❖ **Have poor relationships with others.** People who blame others because they have a false sense of their strengths and their weaknesses will not be in good relationship with other people. If you possess these characteristics, people are not going to want to be around you anyway. It is what you project; it is what you give off. For example: If you work, you either negatively or positively affect your environment. So if you have been from job to job or church to church where you are always belittling people or being critical of people, chances are it is because you need to change something. God is not pleased with you walking around feeling devalued and placing that blame on other people. Look at Paul and Barnabas. Barnabas had an alliance with John Mark, who forsook them on a previous mission (Acts 15). Because of his attachment, he left the company of one of the greatest apostles in history for an unfaithful "friend." Leave those who may hinder you, and cling to those who have the power to help develop you.

- ❖ **Are extremely sensitive to criticism.** If you are one of those individuals that nobody can say anything to you without you getting upset – this is not healthy. Not all criticism is bad. There is constructive (good) criticism and you should welcome that. But you can only welcome that if you value who it is that you are. As a person of God, you should be in a posture and a position to want to be held accountable, to allow people to speak into your life and help you change your situation. You should allow people to help you get out of your mess, so that you can become more like Him. You are not in this race for you; you are in this race for Him. You are trying to reach the mark (to press towards the mark), and when people come to you, don't be super sensitive and easily offended. Super sensitivity is a sign of immaturity, and it is time for us to get off the milk and onto the meat, so that God will entrust more to us. God has given us gifts, talents, and abilities, and He is looking for us to make a return on the investment He has made in us. When we gripe and feel "less than" and sorry for ourselves, God is not getting a return on His investment. We must take responsibility for all God has entrusted to us. You cannot be sensitive to criticism as in the case of Ahab in I Kings, chapter 16. His inability to deal with not getting his way resulted in him losing the kingdom.

❖ **Give up when a task becomes difficult.** God does not make quitters. He makes people who are willing to connect to Him (those who desire to be victorious), change, and overcome. If you are going to be the head and not the tail, you cannot have the word *quit* in your vocabulary. When people have low esteem and someone comes to hold them accountable, they feel as though this person is pressing them or moving in on their territory, so they quit and run. That is not God's plan for your life. He wants you to operate on a higher level of esteem and know that if you quit now, when you get to the next place that you are going, you will still have the same issues. When you quit, God cannot come in and change your situation. You are basically saying, "You know that I am not going to follow the plan, instructions, or blueprint that you give me; I am just going to sit and wait for something to happen." You must believe that "God want you to be empowered to stay in the race and go all the way through. So, decide today to stay in the race and to finish the course like Paul (Acts 20).

❖ **Are more likely to succumb to peer pressure; they cannot handle stress and are afraid to try new things.** When is the last time that God spoke to you and instructed you to do something new? You knew it was the voice of God, but you allowed your soulish man (your carnal man) to rule and to win. You did not take action and because of that you missed a divine opportunity. You have to face your fears. Get out there and dare to make things happen. God has not given you the spirit of fear, but of power, the motive force behind something making it effective. So in everything you do, do it with power and a sound mind, loving all people in all things that you do.

We should not succumb to peer pressure; we should be able to overcome pressure. God has not called us to manage stress, He called us to overcome in all things, stress included. Saul was the shining example of not resisting peer pressure (I Samuel, chapters 9-15). He was a people pleaser. Though handsome and powerful, he had some cracks in his personal esteem foundation. He, too, lost his kingdom and his family. What price are you willing to pay for healthy esteem? Maybe you should add up what it is costing you not to have healthy esteem?

- ❖ **Do not have fun.** The Bible says a merry heart doeth good like medicine, and that the joy of the Lord is my strength. You must understand that God came so that you can enjoy life and be a good representative. Be like Jesus, go to a wedding and have fun. Get on a yacht, row to the other side, and go away by yourself – do something!

People with positive (healthy) esteem typically:

- ❖ **Have good relationships with others.** When Jesus becomes your focus, your identity crisis will end. You will learn how to take the focus off yourself and place it on others. Then you will focus on wanting to please God and being in relationship with Him. God has commanded you to love your neighbor as yourself, so you have to be in right relationship with other people. You have to purpose in your heart that you are not going to gossip, talk maliciously, or exemplify the fruits of a carnal nature, but you are going to live according to the Word of God. When you desire to have God's esteem, there is no place for you in you. Make sure that His image is exemplified in all that you do.

- ❖ **Are not overly afraid of new situations.** It is a matter of your perception. Do not look to the left or the right, but look to God who is the author and the finisher of your faith. You cannot allow anything to distract you. You cannot allow anything to cause you not to walk in what God has preordained for your life.

When you get in that place, you must start speaking the Word of God over that situation. You have to encourage yourself by saying, "God you have not given me a spirit of fear, but of peace, love and a sound mind," so that you can make sound, godly decisions and choices. Like David encouraged himself, we too must encourage ourselves.

We normally do not think that way, so when we get into the midst of situations, we allow them to overtake us. When you are walking into a window of opportunity that is God-given and God-directed, because you listened to Him and trusted Him to see you through, you will come out victorious on the other side. Only people with low esteem get in the middle and start sinking, because they took their eyes off Him and put it on their circumstances.

As you develop healthy esteem, you must learn that looking at your circumstances should not be part of your make-up or character. You have to learn how to let new situations fuel you to walk in the divine blessings of God. There may be times when you do not feel worthy, but feel "less than," which means that you are simply focused upon yourself, and you are not allowing the God man in you to be brought forth.

When everything, whether positive or negative, is about you, it is pride. Pride can masquerade in many forms; it ranges from arrogance to having a pity party. Anything that causes you to turn your focus off God will stifle you and cause you to feel 'less than'. As a child of God, you must be able to walk into those new situations with confidence and boldness. The Bible says that we must persevere!

- ❖ **Are able to share of their time, talent, and resources.** They are able to give freely. They are not selfish and they do not hold on or hoard everything to themselves. People with low self-esteem do not want to share anything. They just want it all to themselves. When you have healthy esteem, you do not mind blessing people and you do not mind sharing what it is that God has done for you. Susanna, Lydia, and the other women who supported Jesus' ministry were giving and selfless individuals (Luke, chapter 8).

- ❖ **Are able to use failure constructively.** Anytime a situation is presented to you, take a moment to ask God how He intends to be gloried by this situation. Even though the enemy meant the situation for evil, you can use it for God's good, no matter what the situation is. How do you use the failures in your life? Stop saying that they are failures and start speaking life! Start saying that these are opportunities for increase, growth, and change in your life! People with healthy esteem understand that! What are you learning from your failures? A person with healthy esteem understands that there is something that God desires them to learn.

- ❖ **Accept their strengths and weaknesses.** People with healthy esteem are able to keep going on a difficult task. There may be times when you are tired and weary, but you have to continue to do what God has instructed you to do so that you can fulfill your destiny and walk in your divine purpose! With God as your strength and your source, He will equip you and empower you! His Word says that He will not give you more than you can handle. Trust His Word, speak those things that are not as though they were and know that He is not here to harm you, but to give you hope for your future! Then you can complete your assignment with the confidence you need to press on. You may have to make some adjustments, but a person with healthy esteem recognizes that there are going to be times when they have to do that. Keep going until God tells you to stop! It does not matter what anybody else around you says. If you know that God said for you to keep going, then endure the course, and stay in the race! You must keep going because He has already promised to bless you abundantly.

- ❖ **Are able to express many different feelings.** People with healthy esteem are able to express feelings and emotions and not be overtaken by them to the point where it discredits who they are or who God is. Do not take out what you are going through on other people. When you are healthy, you will recognize that there are times when God will have you say nothing at all. It is then that you should get on your knees and let your supplications be known unto Him so that He can handle His business. People with healthy esteem have fun, enjoy life, and know how to express it!

Were you able to determine if you have negative or healthy esteem? Read through this chapter again and list the things you need to change personally. Then, think about the steps you are willing to commit to in order to be healthy in your esteem? Write out your personal action plan below:

_____
_____
_____
_____
_____
_____
_____
_____
_____
_____
_____
_____
_____
_____
_____
_____
_____
_____
_____
_____
_____
_____

Chapter Seven

How Do I Develop Healthy Esteem?

Renew Your Mind

Philippians 2:5, "Let this mind be in you that is also in Christ Jesus."

If it is not your goal to have the mind of Christ, then you are not going to be on a journey towards becoming healthy. In order to become healthy and have healthy esteem, He desires that you have the mind of Christ. It is mandated that you must adapt your attitude to Christ's attitude.

> **Romans 12:2, "Do not conform any longer to this pattern of this world but be transformed to the daily renewing of your mind."**

It is a daily renewing. We are to deny ourselves, take up our cross, and follow Him daily, because He wants our mind constantly renewed. There is a progression that occurs when you say, "God, renew my mind. Transform me."

Put God First

Destroy everything that you think about yourself. Anything that is under the category of negative esteem has to go, because it is considered self. We must decide to be God focused. God esteem will increase you. It is going to catapult you to the next level, strengthen you, and help you take on the fruit of the spirit. God esteem will allow you to walk in love and gentleness, not anger and frustration. Anger and frustration are not of God. Put God first and destroy everything that is not like Him.

> *Isaiah 43:18-19, "Forget the former things; do not dwell on the past. See, I am doing a new thing! Now it springs up; do you not perceive it?"*

God wants to do a new thing in your life, but if you are constantly walking in negative esteem and you are stuck in the past, you are not going to get to that new thing that He desires for you. Forget about the former life. God said do not dwell in the past. If you are dwelling in the past, you are dealing with negative esteem.

Make a Quality Decision to Change and Become Consistent

Make a quality decision that you are going to lead a wholesome life in Christ, taking on His character and attributes. Then decide that you will become consistent. Consistency is a uniformity of successive events. Succession is something that should become a pattern in your life. Uniformity is: the more you do it, the more you become like that. Become consistent in your mind. Your mind is the place of understanding and intellect. You have to become stable and consistent.

Proverbs 4:5-7, "Get wisdom, get understanding and do not forget thy words or swerve from them. Wisdom is supreme; therefore get wisdom. Though it cost all you have, get understanding."

God wants you to be passionate about pursuing wisdom. What are you thinking about as a person of God? You cannot think about crazy, messy stuff and be consistent in your mind. Whatever is excellent or praiseworthy, that is what you have to think on!

Become consistent in your words. Words are meaningful sounds or combination of sounds.

Proverbs 23, "For as a man thinketh in his heart so is he."

Learn the vocabulary for success. If you are to be successful, then you are to avail yourself to the things that are necessary for you to become successful.

Become consistent in your actions. Action is a state or process of doing. It is vigorous activity.

> **Philippians 4:8,** *"Whatever you have learned or received or heard from me or seen in me, put it into practice."*

Everything that you hear and read about the Word of God, you must learn to activate in your life by putting it into practice. Then the peace of God will be with you. What you do right now will determine your future; therefore, you must learn to take action now.

Learn to Evaluate Yourself and Constantly Take an Inventory of Where You Are

If you do not take an inventory of where you currently are, you will not be able to increase. You must know what you need to increase and improve upon. In order to set goals to achieve more, you have to identify what you must learn, and then you can set your goal and develop a plan to achieve the goal. If you never stop and pause to see where you are in your life, you will never know what God will have you pursue.

Get Away from Corrupt People

Bad company corrupts good character. If we believe the Word of the Lord, then we have to be obedient.

I Corinthians 15:33, "Don't be fooled by those who say such things; if you listen to them you will start acting like them."

Corrupt people will cause you to slip back into that low self-esteem, and once you slip back into that low esteem, you re-enter the world of unhealthiness. If left in this negative state, you become critical and judgmental of everyone else's high esteem, which is not of God. You must guard and protect your God esteem.

Rejoice in Spite of Your Circumstance, Regardless of What you are Going Through

James 1:2-5, "Consider it pure joy, my brother, whenever you face trials of many kinds, because you know that the testing of your faith develops perseverance."

Perseverance must finish its work so that you can be mature and complete, not lacking anything. You must persevere until the end! God requires it as part of the process.

Make it a Practice to Desire Good Morals

Matthew 5:8, "God blesses those whose hearts are pure, for they will see God."

God said, "Be holy for I am holy." You cannot stay in sin and expect God to bless you. He wants to see you desiring holiness and righteousness.

Romans 12:1, "Therefore I urge you, brothers, in view of God's mercy to offer your bodies as living sacrifices, holy and pleasing to God; this is your spiritual act of worship."

Your act of worship is a life that is set aside, consecrated, pleasing, and holy to God. You represent the kingdom to other people. When they see you walking in the full power and image of Him reflected by your lifestyle, then they will be drawn to that, and you will cause all men to come unto Him.

My Personal Power Principles
I will (create your list of what you will do):
_____

Example: I will put GOD first no matter what!
_____
_____
_____
_____
_____
_____
_____
_____
_____
_____
_____
_____
_____
_____
_____
_____
_____
_____
_____
_____
_____
_____
_____
_____
_____

Chapter Eight

The Power of Healthy Esteem

Once you start to understand that everything you have need of is already within, you can start operating in the power of healthy esteem. Remember, if we are to utilize this greatness (power) in all that we do, we must have the confidence and assurance of knowing who we are. God desires for you to be healthy and whole! He desires for you to understand that you are fearfully and wonderfully made! He desires for you to have healthy esteem! Healthy esteem brings about the power of God's increase for your life. Therefore, we must have a healthy image, because it is God's plan for your life. Increase is God's desire for you!

In conclusion, as you recognize the power of healthy esteem, you must acknowledge that God wants you to continually operate in His power by increasing and being empowered in these areas:

Knowledge

You must understand that your journey through life is sustained by the power of knowledge. Knowledge builds confidence. Knowledge gives you the power to know yourself and God's plan for your life. It will allow you to understand what He has in His plan for your purpose and destiny. Then you will be able to set your goals, walk in your divine purpose, and pursue your destiny.

Knowledge helps you to acquire healthy esteem!

I WILL ACQUIRE THE RIGHT KNOWLEDGE!
I WILL SEEK UNDERSTANDING!
I WILL SET GOALS!
I WILL PURSUE MY PURPOSE!
I WILL REACH MY DESTINY!

Confidence

Confidence is one of the invisible powers that enables you to accomplish the impossible. Only with God are all things possible. When you recognize that He is the One who empowers you, you will be able to accomplish the impossible. Confidence helps you to achieve your goals. Confidence helps you to acquire healthy esteem!

I BELIEVE THAT WITH GOD ALL THINGS ARE POSSIBLE! I CHOOSE TO BELIEVE IN POSSIBILITY!

Positive Attitude

You may have to fake it until you make it. You may have act like it until you have it. When you understand that God's provision and His plan for your life is for you to have healthy esteem, then your attitude must change. When your attitude is adjusted to be healthy, then it sets off things medically in your body that will increase your confidence and joy level. It will affect how you carry yourself. Look to God as your absolute source to supply your needs, and say, "God, change my mind, change my attitude. I am willing to be used by You and I surrender every part of my being to You." When we have the joy of the Lord, it sends signals to every other part of our body and causes immediate change. Make certain that you are allowing God to operate and elevate your faith level. Make it a practice to think positive at all times. You will become whatever you think. Practice positive thoughts to get positive results. A positive attitude helps you to acquire healthy esteem!

I WILL HAVE A POSITIVE ATTITUDE!

Mediation or Reflection

You have to see yourself with healthy esteem. Your thoughts will manifest into actions, and actions will manifest into results. Reflect on what you need to become, and see that whole progression in action. When your inner and outer life is in proper alignment, you should be responsive, obedient, and committed to the Word of God. Then you will have the inner strength to endure. That is God's plan for your life. Your power is in your healthy esteem. What is your esteem like? Meditation helps you to acquire healthy esteem!

I WILL MEDITATE AND THINK ON GOOD THINGS!

Now, take on the healthy esteem that God desires you to have so that you can be all that God has called you to be!

There is power in healthy esteem!!

My Personal Power Principles
_____
_____
_____
_____
_____
_____
_____
_____
_____
_____
_____
_____
_____
_____
_____
_____
_____
_____
_____
_____
_____
_____
_____

My Personal Power Principles

_____
_____
_____
_____
_____
_____
_____
_____
_____
_____
_____
_____
_____
_____
_____
_____
_____
_____
_____
_____
_____
_____
_____
_____
_____

My Personal Power Principles

My Personal Power Principles